Happy Holidays!

HAPPY VALENTINE'S DAY!

By Alex Appleby

Gareth Stevens Publishing

Please visit our website, www.garethstevens.com. For a free color catalog of all our high-quality books, call toll free 1-800-542-2595 or fax 1-877-542-2596.

Library of Congress Cataloging-in-Publication Data

Appleby, Alex.
Happy Valentine's Day! / by Alex Appleby.
p. cm. — (Happy holidays!)
Includes index.
ISBN 978-1-4339-9953-6 (pbk.)
ISBN 978-1-4339-9954-3 (6-pack)
ISBN 978-1-4339-9951-2 (library binding)
1. Valentine's Day — Juvenile literature. I. Appleby, Alex. II. Title.
GT4925.A66 2014
394.2618—d23

First Edition

Published in 2014 by
Gareth Stevens Publishing
111 East 14th Street, Suite 349
New York, NY 10003

Editor: Ryan Nagelhout
Designer: Sarah Liddell

Photo credits: Cover, p. 1 OlegDoroshin/Shutterstock.com; p. 5 © iStockphoto.com/ssj414; p. 7 © iStockphoto.com/fotostorm; pp. 9, 24 (hearts) © iStockphoto.com/nkbimages; p. 11 © iStockphoto.com/kirin_photo; pp. 13, 24 (valentines) auleena/Shutterstock.com; p. 15 Digital Vision/Thinkstock.com; p. 17 jsmith/E+/Getty Images; p. 19 © iStockphoto.com/Imagesbybarbara; pp. 21, 24 (roses) wjarek/Shutterstock.com; p. 23 © iStockphoto.com/Zorah.

Printed in the United States of America

CPSIA compliance information: Batch #CW14GS: For further information contact Gareth Stevens, New York, New York at 1-800-542-2595.

Contents

Valentine's Day
is a fun holiday.

BE
MINE

It is on February 14.

It is a holiday
about love!

Snake Facts
Cottonmouth

Length	24 to 48 inches (61 to 122 cm)
Weight	2 to 4 pounds (0.9 to 1.8 kg)
Where It Lives	southeastern United States
Life Span	not known for sure; oldest known cottonmouth was almost 25 years old
Killer Fact	The cottonmouth has a nasty bite, but some prey bite back! When that happens, the cottonmouth bites quickly and lets the prey run away. The snake follows the prey until it dies. Then it eats the prey.

We give gifts to people.

People give out cards.
These are valentines.

LOVE
happy valentine's day
MINE
YOU ARE MY

Many cards look
like little hearts.

Some people
give flowers.

Many people get roses.

Red roses mean love!

Blue roses are
for friends!

Words to Know

hearts

roses

valentines

Index

I LOVE
YOU!